AVALGAR

To my wife Susan,
my companion and friend.

© Andrew Rice-Oxley 2007
Amendments July 2010

Published by ARO Books UK

ISBN 9 7809546 13921

AVALGAR

AND OTHER POEMS

Poems of faith, doubt and hope

Andrew Rice-Oxley

ARO

CONTENTS

AVALGAR
AND OTHER POEMS

Consort both heart and lute, and twist a song
                              Pleasant and long:
Or, since all music is but three parts vied
                              And multiplied,
O let thy blessed Spirit bear a part
And make up our defects with his sweet art.

(George Herbert, *Easter*)

These fragments I have shored against my ruins

(T.S. Eliot, *The Waste Land*)

AVALGAR

At last we came to Avalgar.

It had been a long and barren journey through space,
Our patience stretched to the limit,
But now our hopes were high
As we approached this distant world
Whose star had beckoned us
Across the black immensity
As if it had some secret to impart.

The planet looked good,
The ground felt firm beneath our feet,
The air was clean,
The light like earth's
Only purer, clearer,
And the land was wondrously fertile.
Rivers and streams ran freely,
Fruits, crops and creatures of many kinds
Flourished in great abundance:
A rich, ripe world it was,
All ready to be plucked and tasted,
And all ours for the taking.

But we were not exploiters or conquerors,
We were enlightened men and women.
We'd learnt the lessons of human history,
All but resolved Earth's economic and environmental ills,
And 'came in peace for all mankind',
Seeking new knowledge and new experience,
Hungering for new forms of happiness,
For life on Earth had grown too dull for us,
Too flavourless. And so it was the *people*
Of this fine new world that we all longed to know –
Those whom we called Avalgarians –
For surely, we thought, whoever inhabits this pure paradise
Must know a joy and liberty unknown to us.

They were a primitive but friendly race
Who smiled with childlike innocence
And welcomed us as angels from on high,
Yet strangely showed no fear of us,

No awe for our greater knowledge and intelligence.

We watched them working on the land by day,
We watched them, in the evening, singing, dancing,
Story-making, living in perfect harmony.
We saw (we thought) contentment shining out
From all their faces
And always our eyes were on them
To discover whence came such deep joy.
They let us watch, they invited us to join them –
But we preferred to observe –
Yet they would not, could not, explain to us
The secret of their happiness.

And then, one day, quite suddenly,
We learnt their lives were not as perfect as we'd thought.
We found they were a repressed race, an inhibited people;
Cowed by empty and irrational fears,
Cut off from a source of harmless pleasure
That was all theirs for the taking
If only they willed.

There it stood, quietly waiting,
At the heart of one of the fairest woods,
Beckoning to us to approach and behold its branches,
Loaded down with ripe, red fruit which winked
At us through lush green leaves and bade us
Pluck and taste to our heart's content.

The Avalgarians looked on with horror
As we reached out to grab
This succulent fruit and sink
Our teeth into its tempting flesh.
They would not eat the fruit.
They claimed that countless other trees
Supplied all their desires and needs
And this one tree they always left alone,
Because of an ancient superstition, some primitive taboo
That would not even let them touch the fruit.
They said their gods forbade it
And would punish them if they transgressed:

Such was their naive belief.
But we, determined to try everything,
And smiling at their quaint folklore,
Did not deny ourselves
And ate quite freely of the fruit.

And straightaway our eyes were opened,
And though we never could repeat the pleasure
Of that first sweet bite,
(It slightly palled on second taste),
The insight that it gave us remained with us for ever.

We saw how flat these Avalgarians were, how dull!
Though they had no crime, no conflict and no bitterness,
Their peace was hollow, their happiness shallow,
They lacked the sharp spirit of adventure and experiment,
Their joys were confined to ordinary things!
These people weren't worth studying or filming,
Who on earth would want to know
Of these lacklustre creatures,
These spineless, insipid primitives,
Who couldn't fight or commit adultery
Because it would never enter their heads?

Had we come all that way just to discover
A race of automatons,
A colourless breed of utter nonentities?
Had all our striving, searching, questing,
All our longing
Come to nothing?

Sick at heart, our high hopes dashed,
We stole away to our waiting ship,
Left that alien world behind us,
And headed back through the blackness
To Earth.

SIN AND GRACE

We threw Sin out of the window once,
In a time of rash confidence,
Never expecting to see him again;
But he slipped back in unknown to us
And hid. We threw Grace out too,
Thinking help no longer needed, Sin gone.
Thus liberated from Sin and Grace, our lives progressed
Delightfully unhampered by guilt and meek dependence:
Uninhibited we were and paying dues to no one.

But Sin hadn't gone, not he.
He lurked, he lingered on invisibly
Amongst our belongings, behind our curtains and chairs,
In undusted cupboards and corners, on the stairs,
Up in the bedrooms, under our very sheets.
Noticed now and yet not recognised,
Like that smell of gas or burning you just cannot trace
And end up trying to ignore.

Yes, Sin, now secure, spread intangible unease
And poisoned all our calm
And we still didn't know he was living in our home!
Only Grace, shut out, faced pressed close to the window pane,
Knew he was there and itched to come at him again;
Longed to beat out, to sweep away the insidious power of Sin,
But all offers went unheeded: we wouldn't let Grace in.

DEJECTION

Walking, walking, walking and wondering,
Wondering *why* I'm walking and wondering,
When I could be elsewhere, working, working
And filling my life with something worthwhile.

Walking, walking, walking and wondering
Why I'm here when I could be with people,
Seeing them laugh and play the fool,
Hearing them talk and talking too.

Walking, walking, walking and wondering,
Soon I stop wondering why,

For people have nothing to say to me,
I have nothing to say to them,
And work could never be worthwhile
When I've lost all heart.

TO MR COOL, THE CELLULOID SAVIOUR

Don't tell me of your bravery
But tell me of your fears;
Don't tell me of your triumphs
But tell me of your tears.

To breeze through life is enviable,
To vault all obstacles is fine,
But can you help me, Superman,
When your experience of life's not mine?

JOB'S WIFE SPEAKS OUT

How many times has the sun toured the earth,
Sightseeing all its disasters and miseries
Without batting an eye?
Out go its rays impersonally
To our helpless world,
Which cannot escape,
Only lose the light for awhile
And briefly forget
How the sun sits up in the heavens
And looks down on all.
Out go its rays, day after day,
Regardless of who is dying or being born;
Out go its rays indiscriminately,
Pouring out pointless energy
On good and bad alike,
Spectating every tremor on earth
Unchanged itself: the smugly sitting
Blinding burning sun.

O sun, sun, brazen, barbarous sun!
Do you ever think what you're doing?
Do you ever think what you're seeing?
To think that you can shine and shine and still not care!

You watch with complete indifference
My family wiped out ... our whole household!
My husband, stripped of all his wealth and prosperity,
Down to the very last rag,
Now suffering hideously in his wretched body
Punishment fit only for the worst blasphemer,
And he so upright, honest and true!

What on earth do you shine *for*,
O brainless sun?
Without justice or purpose,
Your light sheds no light,
Is worse than the dark,
And all the innocent sufferer can do,
Though Job will not (and God knows why),
Is curse your Almighty, 'merciful' Maker
And make Him destroy the life that He gave.

RESPONSES TO LIFE'S TRIALS AND TRIBULATIONS: HUMAN AND DIVINE

Jesus went out as usual to the Mount of Olives [to the Garden of Gethsemane] and his disciples followed him. On reaching the place, he said to them. "Pray that you will not fall into temptation." He withdrew about a stone's throw beyond them, knelt down and prayed, "Father, if you are willing, take this cup from me; yet not my will but yours be done." An angel appeared from heaven and strengthened him. And being in anguish, he prayed more earnestly, and his sweat was like drops of blood falling to the ground. (Luke 22, 39-44). *Then everyone deserted him and fled* (Mark 14, 50).

It's easy to numb the sensitive place,
To make life's troubles seem faint and remote,
To sink your worries in a barrel of ale,
Or seek some other sedative,
Forgetting them all.
It's easy, but it won't resolve
A single problem you face.

It's easy enough to shrug your shoulders,
To slump heavily into a chair,
Draw a blind down in your mind,
Pretending that the world's not there.
It's easy, but it doesn't succeed in erasing anyone's care.

It's tragically easy to 'jack it all in',
Surrender yourself to gloom and despair:
Too easy, but it doesn't get you anywhere
For despair is a bottomless pit ...

It's all too easy to glare around you,
Putting the blame on somebody else,
Lay all the world's ills at a foreign door,
To gawp, then carp at the sins over there,
Be filled with a glow of self-righteousness,
Saying, "You'll never catch *me* doing that!"
It's easy, but it doesn't improve the state of the world one jot.

It's easy to lash out against opposition
When your enemy is weak or in the wrong,
To hit back hard against accusation
When you know your case is strong.

It's easy, but it doesn't touch the cause of the spite.
Like a strong stick slashing through stinging nettles,
It brings a tremendous feeling of triumph
But it fails to get to the root of the threat.

****

It was hard for Christ
In the garden that night –
Alert, sober, aware –
Hard for him to be fully awake and choose
To look straight at the horror to come.
It was hard for him to hold himself up,
To say and mean, "Thy will be done".
It was hard for him, how hard for him,
In the bloody sweat of that glaring garden
But he gained an answer and carried on.

It was hard for him to witness the fall
Of all in his closest company,
The treachery and faithlessness
Of those whom he especially loved.
It was hard for him to be left alone
In the cold, malevolent night,
And not condemn his fickle friends.
It was hard for him to be forgiving,
But it left a way open for their return.

It was hard for him to listen to lies,
To be falsely accused for all his good deeds,
To suffer the rancour, the meanness, the spite,
The lashes, the lashes, the lashes, the lashes,
And the stabbing thorns around his head!
The soldiers' moronic, mindless mockery,
The demented mob's sadistic howls,
Pilate's pathetic washing of his hands.

It was hard for him to be gashed with nails,
To be hammered down on a slab of wood,
Then hauled up to endure the taunts,

15

The sneers and the jeers of those righteous men.
It was hard for him, so hard for him,
Not to hit back when he knew that he had
Not only right but might on his side,
Hard for him to show he was God
By not showing he was God;
Hard for him to take all the hate
And the stinging scorn that was hurled at him,
Take it and absorb it all
Until it was drained and shrivelled up.
It was hard for him to face the void,
To plumb the infinite depth of sin,
To know the despair of losing the One
Who had borne him up in everything,
To know that despair, yet not stop loving.

It was hard to die
Not *seeing* the victory.

It was hard, hard,
Harder than we'll ever know

But it worked.

It broke the cycle of evil
And the power of death,
Reversing the *fall*.

Opened up for good
The way back to God,
The healing of the world,
Of us all.

LUST AND LOVE

Lust is easy,
Love is hard;
Lust is hasty,
Love takes time.
Lust would have everything now,
Lust grabs and gulps,
Then spits it out.

Love demands nothing,
Will wait with open, empty hands,
And whatsoever it receives,
Be it ever so small,
That will it keep and cherish as if all.

Lust is a push-button pleasure,
Only seven seconds to satisfaction:
'All you have to do' is mechanically prod
A semi-dormant fantasy,
The rest is automatic.

Love is a strenuous, painstaking joy
And seventy times seven months
Still leaves it far from its high mark,

Oh, lust is a self-important spark
Whose vanity's soon snuffed

But love is an enduring flame
Which steadfastly stands up again
After every shaking
And holds its course
In STILLness.

HOLLOW DEPRESSION?

Malice inhabits our universe:
Malice and Envy.
The Evil One cannot abide
Fair weather, clear skies.
He seethes with discontent
At love and joy and hope and health;
The smallest spark of kindness
Stings him to the heart.

So be not dismayed
When a wave of resentment rises within
At some very petty wrong.
When shadows of regret
Threaten the bright memory
Of a joy that was never meant to stay.
When blankness and despondency
Fall around you mysteriously, irrationally.
It is only the Enemy, showing his hand,
Trying to grab the initiative again,
Playing his few trumps while he can.

Be not dismayed, rather rejoice and laugh!
Those brooding clouds of blackness
Manufactured from mere dust within
Show clearly that Satan is panicking,
Just kicking up a smokescreen.
He knows his trumps won't last,
His tricks are few and far between,
That a mightier Hand than his
Rules the vast universe
And all that therein is.
He's going for a quick, cheap victory,
Furious, frustrated, desperate;
Knowing that in the end he cannot win,
Knowing that he may blot and blur and mar and stain,
Perplex and jar the surface,
But never touch the solid core of God's Good,
Knowing that, despite his clever, calculating game,
All his efforts, all his 'work',
Only serve to make us value more
That which he would destroy.

Satan Replies

Laugh at your peril, you puny human!
That 'mere dust' you scoff at,
Will dog and bug you all your life
And be the death of you.
Never forget, you arrogant speck,
That your mortality will always
Make a mess of you.
You'll always lack firm self-control:
Time and again you'll be angry, frustrated,
Let a depression creep up on you
And blot out all your good intent.
And when that happens, as happen it will,
I'll be the one to laugh not you.
'Mere dust' indeed!
That dust will rise and rise again
And choke your brash disdain.
Face the truth, fear me, give me my due,
And one thing you'll not suffer from
Is self-delusion. Go on, give in,
Accept your fallibility.
Be honest with yourself,
Admit you cannot win.

The Lord Speaks

Be silent, both of you!
You are both right and yet
You both omit the vital truth:
Christ died and rose again.
The dust is defeated
But it is only 'mere dust'
Because of my Son's work.
Discount that work
And the dust will indeed
Dog and bug and choke to death
As Satan claims.
Beware of pride, O child of mine.
Never try to bypass
Your Redemption.

SATANIC INCARNATION IN PULP FICTION AND THE MOVIES

So now our search
For the sordid and sensational
Has reached its ultimate, sterile depth.
Satan is imagined incarnate
For our macabre delight.
He has burrowed into human flesh
To work his evil will,
Corrupting, perverting, depraving,
Wreaking ruin and spreading torment
From within the confines of one human form,
Living at one point in time,
Born of a particular mother,
In one particular society –
Just like Jesus Christ –
The precise Anti-Christ.

What a startling theme,
What challenging stuff!
Something to make the Christians think,
And, moreover, the sort of thing the public likes
And is bound to lap up
After its stomach has recovered
From the last film shocker.

But O my shallow-minded friends,
Who can seriously believe it?
What sort of home would Satan choose
Had he the power to become incarnate?
Certainly not a stable or humble dwelling place –
Too tough by half.
What then? A palace?
Clothed in finest linen, coddled in luxuries
All his growing life, causing anguish and stress,
Creating conflict all around him,
Himself cosily cushioned from it:
Out Heroding-Herod, Hitler, Stalin, Pol Pot?
The picture would appear to fit,
And think of the spectacular scenes of cruelty
The eye might feast upon
In high definition, super-technicolor!

But wait. Lay down those twitching cameras,
Still the itching eye and finger, staunch
The gathering saliva, and think again.
Herod, Hitler, Stalin, Pol Pot,
For all their earthly power
Could never fully numb
The pain and sensitivity of being human.
Could Satan, would Satan face that too?
Risk human vulnerability,
A host of unpredictable emotions,
Even pity and love?

No. Better far to stay in the shady *spirit* realm,
Making sorties into the human sphere,
Spreading poison here and there,
Planting vicious bombs of malice,
Then retreating to a safe place
To view the damage done.
Always out of range, looking on,
Never actually involved in the suffering caused,
Therefore never touched by dangerous
Compassion, grief or guilt.

Isn't this more like Satan?
Doesn't this more truly fit?
The scheming demon, disguised
As a human being, perhaps,
(Diabolic docetism),
But a man, a real *man*?
Can you really see him
Expose himself to feel
'The heartache and the thousand natural shocks
That flesh is heir to'?

Why, he wouldn't have the guts!

ON AN EIGHT YEAR OLD RUN OVER

It was rotten luck –
He only wanted to cross the road.

A main road, true, and at night,
But there were fewer cars about than in daylight
And hundreds of kids had done it before
And been all right.

If only the car had been going a little bit slower
Or he'd been running just a little bit faster!
Where was God then? Couldn't He
Have arranged one or the other
Or even the presence of a father or mother?

He was only trying to cross the road:
Such a small and innocent endeavour.
Did he deserve to pay with his life
When it was only rotten luck?

THE SCHOOL CARETAKER

He wasn't a very cultured man
He wasn't a great conversationalist
He wasn't an expert on anything,
But he was a man you could talk to.

He wasn't a very successful man
His job was hum-drum
His prospects had always been few
He didn't hob-nob with the well-to-do,
He was a man anyone might talk to.

He wasn't a charismatic man:
His looks were not striking
He did not have a strong personality
Nor did his presence *demand* respect
And yet
When you looked into his open face
And saw his kind attentive eyes,
You could tell
He was a man you could talk to.

He wasn't a man who was greatly esteemed
By the world or very much noticed
By those at the top.
True, when he retired, the new Headmaster referred
To his 'longstanding service' in his end of term speech
(He allocated him a whole sentence).
He received a present 'From the School'
And several older teachers and staff were truly sad
To see him go; yet, for many, his leaving
Was not a matter of much significance.

Only certain children down the years
Could really know what his going meant;
Inconsequential children, confused and rather forlorn,
Who, stealing down long drab corridors in their free time,
Had sought him out.
They knew
He was a man you could talk to.

THE NEW BOY

He was blubbering on his desk
In the empty form room,
Head buried in his folded arms
As if they were the only place
Where comfort could be found
So far from home.

The teacher looked on helplessly,
Caught in the no-man's land between
Self-interest and sympathy.
Homesickness was terrible, he knew,
He'd suffered too at school,
But what on earth could he do now
At the weary end of a tedious day
When he only wanted to get away?
He'd stay for just a minute or two,
To show the lad he cared,
That someone cared for him,
Then pass the matter on
And hurry home.

The teacher lay in bed that night
Reviewing the long day's turmoil;
The pang brought on by the sobbing boy
Had dulled now to a vague unease
Lost amidst his other cares.
He snuggled up to his sleeping wife,
He was troubled but at least he was home.

The weeping boy was awake in the dorm
Amidst a roomful of sleeping strangers,
Torturing himself with thoughts of the place
Where he wasn't and yet longed to be.
The haven of the holidays was as far away to him
As the sure, firm land to the non-sailor
Caught on a squally sea,
As far away and unbelievable
As a warm June day in an ice-bound January.
He lay locked in misery,
A helpless prisoner of his grief,
Serving what seemed a life sentence;

Hating the thought of the daylight ahead
Which would only expose his tears to the world,
Yet wanting the new day to come:
Hoping and praying that with the morning
There'd be a letter from home.

OUR BIBLE

In one corner of the empty classroom,
Sprawled face down upon the floor,
Its cover half wrenched from the pages,
Lay a hardback copy of the New English Bible:
One derelict Bible,
A not unfamiliar sight in school.

I heard a voice say:
"Throw it away!
It isn't needed any more."

I picked it up and turned it over;
Tried to straighten out the crumpled pages,
Noticing the dirt smeared across the exposed print,
Noting too the other pages, dusty round the edges,
But bearing still that unmistakable, *un*used, *un*read look;
And, unlike the school hymn book, unwritten on,
As if there was no point.
One redundant, hardback Bible:
Fresh from the press two months ago,
Now only ready for the bin.

"Throw it away!
The young and lively, vigorous mind
That knocked it down
Has other things to think about
And doesn't need it anymore!"

Once, one verse alone
Could sustain the sagging spirit;
One page gave a taste of paradise,
One chapter made a feast.
But when you have more exciting fare –
Pulp fiction and videos and spicy magazines –
The Bread of Life seems drab and dull
And isn't inspiring any more.

In thousands of homes throughout the land
Responsible adults respect the Bible.
It isn't manhandled or thrown about,
But is treated as an honourable relic;

Has its appointed place on the shelves
And is never touched, save by a duster.

"Who reads it now,
Who needs it now?
You might as well throw it away!"

Once, people fought for a word of it,
Died for a line of it,
Still do in other lands.
Clutched it to them like a loved one.
Did terrible things in its name, true, some people,
Reading their evil into it,
But it filled many too with great love and great vision.
Now we shun unseemly extremes
And have put it away, feeling
It isn't suitable anymore.

I looked at the page that had had its face
So peremptorily rubbed in the floor
And my eye fell on a gospel passage:
The parable about the wonderful banquet
And the guests who wouldn't come.
The end of the passage was obscured by dirt
And difficult to follow ...

"Well what does it matter? Where is the loss?
The whole book's out of touch today.
Never mind the modern translation,
It just isn't relevant anymore,
"THROW IT AWAY!"

No, I thought, I won't throw it away,
Though battered it be and neglected,
There's life in it yet!
I took the reject out with me,
Closing the door
On the classroom's dismal emptiness.

UNKNOWING HAUNTERS
On Looking at School Centenary Photographs

We've seen the pictures of young lads in uniform
From Great War days, with 'killed in action'
Baldly stated underneath and simple dates
Bluntly proclaiming their brief lifespans;
And every time the tragedy, waste, brutality of war strikes home.

But other photos from the past can touch me too,
Without that moral shock, it's true, but no less poignantly.
Those public school photos showing lads
Whom death has taken too, not prematurely,
But taken nevertheless through mere course of time.
Even the youngest in these photographs, eight or nine years old, perhaps,
Have surely passed on now into the dark or another life.

Their cut of hair and style of clothes
Suggest another age; but oh their faces, their faces,
Despite their mainly blank expressions,
So real, so human, individual, every one of them,
Like those we know or feel we might have known
Had we been living then: acquaintances, or friends even,
But still themselves, utterly themselves, and of their own time.

They sit or stand in serried groups, all looking at the camera,
Very much alive, then, thinking only of their present or immediate future –
What's for tea or supper, what homework's due tomorrow?
Perhaps some let their minds rove further forward
Into the unknown, endless-seeming tracts of time ahead.

They sit or stand there still, caught in time yet out of time,
Looking at us now, not knowing they are dead.

THE FACT OF DEATH

Death is not the corpse laid out before us,
Nor the discreet place where it's conveyed
Whilst our imaginations look away.
It is not the ancient, earthy graveyard
Nor modern crematorium so chillingly efficient;
Nor is it to be found in the social garb
Cast decorously around it in such ponderous ways.
The funeral. Slow, pompous hearse, trimly clad
With formal flowers. Dark attire with sober face.
The mumbled, awkward words of relatives and friends.
The inadequate ceremonial script
And tense, embarrassed, cue-less silence
Hanging heavily over all.
This is not death,
This is just a cloak, a mask.
We need not fear this stiff charade.

But when the show is over,
Then Death emerges in his true blank colours.
He is that clinging absence that will not go away,
That stark, gaunt emptiness
That cannot be covered or filled,
The ache that has no anodyne.
For Death means separation
From those we love, and nothing
Changes that on earth.
It may not, nay it cannot, last forever:
No burial or burning can wipe a person out
And reduce her, him, to a mere 'loving memory'.
Death's division is not final.
But every moment that it lasts is too long
And while it lasts it hurts.

POWER LINES

Forests clothed the land, the towering tree was King:
Provided ships, houses, carriages, furniture, fuel ...
Legend and myth.

But it wasn't sufficient for the human race.
Trees were cut down for crops, industry, 'development',
The landscape denuded in the process,
Stripped
Of its ancient mystic powers and presences.

Then came the robot invasion of our land –
The cloned infantry –
Tall, thin, steely, see-through figures,
Fleshless, soul-less giants,
Grotesque parodies of the human form:
Ridged or pointed, narrow, empty heads,
Double or triple tiers of fixed, broad shoulders,
Stiff, straight, hanging coils for arms,
No hands,
Wired, harnessed together in single file,
By the arm stumps. Motionless, yet stretched out
As far as the eye could see striding the landscape,
Equally indifferent to human habitation and the natural world,
Strung out across suburbs and fields, stalking
Along valleys, rivers, railways, over motorways and moors,
Presences 'not to be put by'; hated
As desecrators, blots, eyesores, a despised,
Sub-human, barbarous race, though serving us;
Much maligned and yet benign,
Blessing us with heat and light and power,
Sustaining us in lives we were happy enough to live.

Forty years on, the robots are gone,
Transmission of power moved underground,
The landscape free of them once more.

An eight year old, searching the past,
Taps in PYLONS on his PC (or the latest gadget),
Brings up their image on the screen and gasps.
Sees monsters, super-humans, aliens, walking the land,
Quizzes his grandfather, "*Were* they like that? And did you really *see* them?"
"Yes," says grandad, surprised by a sudden nostalgia,
"I saw them, couldn't ignore them, they towered up everywhere."
"Wow!" says the child, and "wow!" again, eyes magnified,
"Wish I'd been there!"

FREE NOW

"We're splitting up," she said, in a matter-of-fact way,
Speaking of a husband who wasn't there;
But the dry, dispassionate tone
Ill-disguised the aching void beneath.

My mind groped for something to hold onto,
Reality seemed to slip a moment,
And I saw a chasm
Open out beneath me too.

Good God, I thought. How has it come to this?
After only a year! She was never one
To do things lightly: disenchantment must
Have deepened into desperation
And made the deed imperative.
Yet, even so, I couldn't bear to think
Of those two lives that had been closely linked
Cut adrift and floating free.

'Free' – this word we honour so highly
Was here a painful mockery.
Yes, they would be free now;
Free to range the open sea of life,
The vast and empty *space* ahead,
Alone,
Searching for somewhere else to dock.

THE CHILD

It was amazing, miraculous,
The look I saw on that sin-ridden countenance,
Sam Wilson's fractious face!

He was a man to steer clear of,
He knew strife better than the palm of his hand,
The inside of prisons better than the walls of his home.
Bitter, angry and belligerent he was,
Smashing himself head first into trouble
Every hour of his turbulent life.

"He'd make a lousy husband," we said, but still
Some mug of a girl took him on, hoping to reform him,
Failing completely from the first day on.

And then came the baby,
Bringing foreboding and shaking of heads.
Nobody then looked for less than disaster,
But they didn't see what I saw
The day Sam Wilson met his son –
Such a look of reverence and awe
I wondered if I'd ever known the man before.
The shepherds must have looked that way
On the first Christmas Day.

Who would have believed that this man whom
Social workers, psychologists, police,
Judges, probation officers and warders –
The whole weight of society and law –
Could scarcely tame
Would come to be mastered by a mere child?

It *was* a miracle.
All that got through to him before was a man-made rod.
This time it was God.

MR PLAY-SAFE TAKES A RISK

"Yes," he said, making one of his rare,
Dry statements, "I have taken note of the sun."
It was a burning, blazing July heat wave
And he'd taken note of the sun.

He preferred to creep down dim corridors,
To inhabit dark corners of unvisited rooms.
"My work mustn't suffer," he used to say,
"I cannot afford distractions of any sort."

But now, *now*, he'd rolled his shirt sleeves half way up,
Revealing six inches of his discreet, white flesh.

Sure, some mighty upheaval had taken place
Within that dead, or dormant soul,
For, he'd 'taken note of the sun'.

KNOW YOURSELF AND BE GLAD

There was a boy
Who would only play centre forward
When he was only meant
To bring on the oranges or drinks at half time.

I say *only* meant to bring on the oranges or drinks
But had he performed that task
Things would have been so different for him
And for others too.

He would not have been dogged
By disappointment and frustration
And continual bouts of bitterness.

He would not have made all
Who knew him uncomfortable
Or downright miserable.

He would not have wasted his life
Head-butting walls instead of walking
Through open doorways.

And, of course, those teams
Would have got their refreshments from him
And maybe played just that little better.

But he *would* play centre forward
Or nothing.
So nothing it was for him
Except despair.

THE NEW MAN

God had got inside of him,
Under his defences,
Had broken through
The hard, firm crust of taut reserve,
He'd built up around him through the years,
And worked him over.

His ever-merciful Spirit had mercilessly massaged
All those tense and restless parts of him
Which functioned ill or not at all.
Had toned and tuned them,
Made them hum and sing,
"God, it's good to be alive!"

Gone now was the knotted brow, the grey air,
The fidgety and frightened look,
The eyes that went nowhere.
A new found serenity
Quietly beamed from the heart of him
Through eyes that always held their aim
And a countenance that seemed to reflect the light of the sun.

Before, he'd flinched at most human contact,
People flitted by him like bats in the twilight.
Now he gave each person that he met
A warm full look,
As if that person mattered to him
And made a difference to his life
Even whilst he spoke or listened.

Some rather enviously thought
He had transformed himself
Through an esoteric life skills course,
That he'd mastered some secret technique
For 'making friends and influencing people'.
Some observed he had become remarkably
Well-adjusted to his social milieu,
Though strangely looking beyond it.

Say what you will,
The truth of the matter
Could only be explained like this:
Once God had got in, under his guard,
He had allowed himself,
Without a single reservation,
To be changed.

OWN GOAL
Looking through the window on a wet, miserable day

You have to feel sorry for it –
The gloom and the doom –
No matter how hard it tries
It never quite manages
To break our spirit.

Oh I know it has its hour, and more,
How it can score!
There are days when the greyness
Grinds on and on,
Most effectively staining
Everything it touches:
The overcast sky refuses to shift,
The downpour continues,
The rain-sodden landscape
Lies limp and trodden down,
A leaden depression deadens all.

But look again,
Beyond the tear-besmattered pane.
What do you notice in those pools
That gather on the ground?

Movement
Rhythm
An irrepressible pulse

Yes,

The rain is dancing in the puddles!

PATIENCE AND FAITH

When day wanes
And twilight comes,
Do not try to force time back
And have the defunct light again.
Do not pine that it is gone,
Nor strain your eyes in the thickening dark
Striving to make them do
What they were never designed to do.

Wait in the dark,
Accept the dark.
Let it deepen and fill out the sky,
Let it take its natural course.
Soon stars will pierce pinpricks of light
In the solid black ceiling above.

Wait in the dark in trust.
There is nothing can keep out the light,
No gloom is sealed so tight
It cannot find a way through.

Wait in the dark in trust and in hope.
You will have light again,
Maybe sooner than you think:
Before the inevitable dawn.

CHRISTMAS CONTACT

Christmas is the time of year
When deadened memory revives
And makes us think of all those lives
We've lost touch with over time
And ought to be concerned for now.

We write our cards to preserve a link,
Yet hardly think to connect the act
With the amazing and colossal fact
That on Christmas Day God became Man
And hallowed every human contact.

So, underneath the Christmas cheer,
The superficial seasonal patter,
There lies the sure and solid truth:
All those we've known will always matter.

CHRISTMAS ONLOOKER

I am on the outside looking in,
And, yes, it is a beautiful scene
The Nativity –
Full of wonder and mystery and awe –
As countless artists have testified.
But, oh, to enter into it,
Into the circle from the stable door,
To share,
With the shepherds and Magi and beasts,
The angels and Joseph and Mary,
The divine love radiating from the Child,
To partake with them of that glow!
Not simply to look, to gaze upon,
But to know.

[*This poem was partly inspired by Rembrandt's painting – 'Adoration of the Shepherds' – a reproduction of which I have on my bedroom wall and is shown on the back cover of this book. It is a naturalistic painting of a realistic stable with realistic people. There are no angels in the picture, just the shepherds, Mary and Joseph, and the baby in the manger. It is dark and shadowy in the stable, night-time, but there are two sources of light illuminating the scene. One source is a lantern, which a tall man is holding, and the other, a stronger source of light, is the manger where Jesus is lying. The miraculous thing about this light emanating from the manger is that it looks perfectly natural, yet it can't be because ordinary babies don't emit visible light! This light is therefore both natural and supernatural like the Incarnation itself.*]

STEP IN AND SHARE: A Meditation

You will know and partake of that glow
When you have made the journey.
None of those pictured in the Nativity
Got there by magic:
They travelled there,
They took a risk to be there.
The shepherds took a huge gamble
Leaving their flocks in the middle of the night
In response to crazy lights and singing.

The Magi must have encountered great difficulties and dangers
Trekking across hostile and alien terrain
With only a star and an inner instinct
To justify their folly.

And Joseph and Mary
Doubtless had their fair share of trouble
Before arriving in the stable
And reaching that supreme moment of the Child's birth,
Away from home and all its relative comforts.
Mary bearing too the strangeness, the weight
Of how it had all come about
As well as the pain of the birth,

And they all had the rest of their lives
To live out.

"A sword will pierce your heart also," says Simeon to Mary,
And certainly the shepherds and Magi too
Faced suffering to come.

Yes, when we look at the Nativity
We see but a moment in time.

We may enter it too
And share in the Incarnation

But time does not stand still
And if we are to share in the Incarnation
We must share too
Christ's life as a man and his Passion.

We cannot stay forever in the stable.

We too must move on, grow up, live, suffer,
Die
Before we enter fully into Eternal Life
And know
Our God – the one true God –
Beyond time
For ever and ever. Amen.

OLD WISE MEN, NEW WISE MEN

Reflections on a Christmas Card

They are travelling towards the infant King
Guided only by a star
But we have the Living Word at hand
To lead us on to God's abode
And need not travel physically to any place.

They were looking for a Lord of power
But did not question the Child's credentials.
They worshipped him and presented their special gifts,
Though he was born of an ordinary woman
And looked just like an ordinary child.

But we who know what became of that child,
We who have been told of Christ's life and death
And his resurrection glory,
Are slow to come and worship him.
I wonder why?

Have we become too complacent,
Has God made Himself too easy to find?

Or is it just that we have travelled so far now
Upright along Progress's self-confident way,
We can no longer simply
Get down on our knees
And pray?

TWO CHRISTMASES

A Child's Christmas

For the twelfth time in her life
She wakes to view the warm, encircling wave
Of nicely wrapped packages destined
To wash benignly over her once more.

Twenty minutes later she's swamped
In Christmas gifts laid bare,
Is wading a little impatiently
Through the discarded wrapping paper
Strewn around her bedroom floor.

Then down the stairs she hastens
To bask in family greetings
And 'thank-yous' all round,
In rooms smothered with Christmas decorations
She barely notices now.
To her entranced mind, the Christmas cards,
Laid out on shelves, mantelpieces, tables,
Are just a blur of vague goodwill.
She knows that grandparents, aunts and uncles,
Cousins, friends, nearby and distant,
And neighbours, have supplied them,
But she cannot now distinguish a single one.
Santa Clauses and holly, infant angels, snow scenes
And cartoon snowmen, lanterns, harps, babes in mangers –
With or without serene Madonnas and bearded Josephs –
Tinselled Christmas trees, oxen, reindeer, mice,
Donkeys, stars, robin redbreasts, sheep,
Victorian scenes and eastern kings with camels,
All jostle and clamour for attention,
Getting none from her. Her eyes
Are drawn to the Christmas tree
And to the presents beneath and around it
Yet to be opened ...

When bedtime comes she sinks into bed
Dizzied and dazed by the festive fare –
She's done nothing but absorb all day.
Food and fun, the thrill of new possessions

Have been hers in abundance,
But, like the Christmas pudding,
They've been too rich: body and mind are saturated,
Weighted down with too much bliss.
Her flood of good fortune has swept away
Most of the magic of the day.
Already the Christmas glow has faded,
The feast has grown cold.

An Old Woman's Christmas

On her seventy-eighth Christmas Day –
Her tenth as a widow –
She wakes yet again in the cold and the dark
And dresses by the light of the single bar
In her old electric heater,
The only sign of life
In the early morning's uncanny stillness.
Gets herself downstairs a little bit laboriously
And settles into her solitary, everyday routine.

Yet she knows well it's Christmas,
Has memories and expectations enough
To make the day a special one.

She remembers the vicar's visit only two days ago;
Offers of Christmas dinner, but 'no-thanks,
She'd prefer to stay at home on her own,
Another house would be too strange'.
And there'd been the carol singers the other night,
She heard them singing one of her favourites,
'In the bleak midwinter'.
Two sprigs of holly on the table, one on the sideboard,
A little knot of mistletoe over the living room clock
And a few Christmas cards suffice
To remind her this is no ordinary day.

At eleven o'clock her ancient radio
Brings her Christmas worship for afar,
She doesn't miss that draughty church.
Her food is plain but her thoughts are not.
Once again her eyes are drawn to the mantelpiece
And feast on three cards there, one in particular.

A full week's acquaintance with these cards
Has not dulled her pleasure in them.
She knows them all by heart:
The pictures' every detail,
The wording of the greetings,
Who printed them, even the price of one of them.
She likes the sketch of the local church,
So 'sensitively done'; likes equally the traditional depiction
Of the Three Wise men and their lofty star.
Would have liked one of Mary and the Baby
But the colour snap of her three grandchildren,
Sent in the form of a Christmas card,
Amply compensates for that.

She eats her fairly simple food
In her rather chilly living room
And thinks of them all across the seas,
Sitting round a steaming roast turkey
With sunshine pouring onto them,
Happy in the knowledge that her parcel to them
Has safely arrived. Though their Christmas dinner
Will have been over hours ago, her presents
Long since opened, she likes to imagine it
All happening again; sorry that they're not
With her now but glad that at least
They're in the world and provide
Abundant food for thought and prayer.
Who knows, maybe she'll see them next year?

When bedtime comes, she clambers once more
Into her husbandless bed, wondering
If he sees her now and knows her thoughts;
For reviewing her store of precious reflections,
A warm wave of joy steals gently upon her.
She has remembered and *been* remembered,
Of that she can be sure: this Christmas Day
Would last her seven months, maybe more.

WHO KNOWS CHRISTMAS?

He knows not Christmas,
Christmas he knows nothing of,
He, who sunk in a soft armchair,
Watches flickering lights on a broad, square screen
With half his eyes. Lapped round with warmth
From central heated room and handy alcoholic drink,
His body in a slump, his mind half paralysed,
He is at rest. He has surrendered without a struggle
To the numbing jollity of the season.
How safe and secure he feels in his cosy, comforting
Semi-oblivion. Nothing is required of him now,
No exertion except for the automatic, muscular movements
Needed for swallowing, inhaling, pulling a cracker,
Lifting a knife, fork, or glass. How happy he is,
How well tuned in to merriment! Giggles and guffaws
Come to him as easily as the turning of a switch
Or the pressing of a button, for every sound
That filters through his half-sealed ears can activate
The loose and sloppy mechanism of thoughtless laughter.
Yesterday and tomorrow and much of today
Have faded away. How easily he laughs with half his being,
Half his mind, while the other half sleeps on.
Perfect peace? The peace of Christmas?

Does *she* know Christmas? She whose heart swells up
In her throat as she sings 'While shepherds watched'
Or 'Hark the herald angels sing', though thinking not
Of those other-worldly beings that the shepherds heard,
For she herself has become a radiant angel in her own eyes,
Rejoicing at the rapturous sound of her own voice,
And 'the little town of Bethlehem' she sings of so joyously
Is not the town that Jesus knew nor today's. It is a fairy tale world
Of twinkling lights, friendly and approving faces
And pretty things, all for her. And as she sings,
The stored up magic of her first remembered Christmas
Breaks from her memory cells, filling her
With that ecstatic glow never known again
In all her later life. The Christmas of *her* past she knows,
But the Christmas of history and what's to come –
'The hopes and fears of all the years'? What can she know of those
Hopes and fears when she's no inkling
Of Time's dark tunnel stretching on without an end in sight?

And does the well-cared for, cosseted child
Know Christmas? He or she who cannot wait
To add to last year's pleasures and possessions;
Who wants nothing truly new, only more of the same.
He whose parents play the part of Santa Claus
So well that the old synthetic man lives on
To scatter goodies carelessly on land
Already thick with windfalls. He or she who knows
Far more of Father Christmas, jingle bells
And tinselled snow and red-nosed rubber reindeer,
Than the Father of Creation; more of the well-appointed
Plastic baby doll than of the powerless flesh
And blood baby, born in a primitive stable
On dirty land, clinging to survival
By a meagre thread, with nothing
But his parents' intangible love
And the immaterial goodwill and worship
Of a few rough animals and shepherds
To see him through. Can the spoilt child
Know Christmas whose staple gifts
Are heavy-duty luxuries which come in bubble-wrap?

Who does know Christmas? Who can know Christmas?
Can anyone know what a feast Christmas is
Who has never starved? Can anyone really know the hope
That Christmas holds who's never known despair?
Can anyone know just how bright those angels were
Who has not 'walked in darkness' and known
The deepest misery? No, no one. No one has ever loved
The dawn as he or she who's spent all night outside
Shivering in the dark, wondering if the dawn
Would ever come.

For those who've come to the end of life,
To the end of hope,
To the end of joy,
God sends a baby boy
So they can start again.

Look at this boy,
You destitute who have written Christmas off

49

As not for you. Christmas *is* for you,
For you as no one else.
This new born child – like every new born child
And something more – speaks home to all
But he speaks most to you:
The greater your darkness, the greater his light.
This is the Gospel. God cannot keep his love
In heaven, nor save it simply for the best on earth.
He comes down at Christmas time,
Down, down, down,
He comes down.
Christ. A mere child,
God's greatest gift,
He comes down.

Down through the fading light
He comes,
Down to all the misfits,
All the failures,
Down to all the 'down and outs',
Down to all the broken minds,
Broken wills, down
To all the hopeless souls
Down
Down
Down
Christ comes
Down

Till

Deep
In the
Darkest pit
Of all,
His love explodes,
Searing through
The Gordian tangles
Of too much thought,
Shattering
The tight, hard, starless fabric

Of despair
That hems the helpless in,
And letting in the glory,
Oh what glory!

And only those who've been in hell,
Who've touched the bottom,
Seen the worst,
Suffered endless-seeming agonies,
Faced total darkness,
Tasted solid pitch.
Only those can truly know
The burning, blinding, battering blaze
Of boundless light and power and joy
That was, and is, in Jesus Christ
On his first day, and theirs,
Christmas Day.

STAR OF NIGHT
'The darkness comprehended it not'

SIRIUS blazes in the night sky,
Fifty thousand billion miles from Earth,
Its light crossing the blackness of space,
Defying the darkness, the debris, the vastness,

Even so ...
Through darkened minds
And overcast, derelict hearts
(Lost, loveless souls)
Their tangled thoughts and overpowering fears,
Horror and guilt and self-disgust,
Hatred and hardness and ingrained bitterness,
Inconsolable sorrows and grief,
The sunken hulks of shipwrecked dreams,
Dense clouds of doubt and deep despair,
The wilderness of broken laws,
Countless centuries of sin,
Aberration, anarchy, blindness,
Sheer chaos and confusion ...
Across the fixed gulf between God and humanity,
The murky past and obscure future,
Comes the light (and love)
Of CHRIST.

SIX PIECES
AFTER GEORGE HERBERT
(1593-1633)

THE MAN AND HIS WORK

God's servant
Exceptional scholar
Ordinary priest
Rare, incomparable poet
Gracious pastor
Excellent musician

Humble preacher
Envoy of heaven
Restorer
Book of Books illuminator
Expression of Christ
Revealer of God's love
Treasure inexhaustible

BEDROCK
('Christ is made the sure foundation')

Joy must run deep within us,
Everlasting as an inexhaustible
Spring in the mountains,
Underlying all our hopes and fears,
Sustaining us when surface life is bleak,

Calming us when storms rage outside,
Helping us to stand firm,
Renewing our crushed spirits,
Inspiring us to carry on,
Secretly whispering to us, "Take heart,
Triumph is assured!"

BECOMING WHAT YOU CONTEMPLATE (Matthew 6, 21)

Where do you travel
When **your** mind is free?
You seek **treasure** of some kind, for sure:
Something which **is** precious to you
And beckons where **there** is hidden pleasure, a secret store
Of gilt-edged joy which **will** compensate, you trust, for all
The tedium and dissatisfaction **your** life is subject to.
But don't you see, my friend, your **heart** and mind
Derive their substance and character, will **be** shaped by, whatever
They pursue? If your prized thing is empty so **also** are you.

THE LIGHT SHINES ON IN THE DARK (John 1, 5)

War, famine and disease, **the** destruction of the earth, pollution,
Grasping greed making **light** of the needs of the poor,
Widespread belief what **shines** is only gold, gold and diamonds,
Rampant crime charging **on**, unchecked, out of control,
Corruption and hypocrisy **in** high, inaccessible places,
Hatred, callous terrorism, **the** tendency to blame others
For all that's wrong, the **dark** side of life which haunts everyone,
The break-up of families **and** ordered, stable communities,
Abuse, neglect, cruelty, **the** breakdown of discipline in school,
No jobs, homelessness, **darkness** of drug addiction, despair,
Cold competition which **has** swept away all loyalty and trust,
Rising tide of trivia and **never**-ending lure of material things,
Degenerate appetites, **quenched** only by sick fantasies, porn,
Poisoning love and, with **it**, the future of the innocent unborn.

MAN'S CONDITION: GOD'S VERDICT (1 John 3, 20)

The doctor sagely shook his head,
"The prognosis isn't good," he said,
"I'll give him just a year or so,
And until then? He shrugged, "More drugs?"

The prison governor looked grave and sad,
"Remission for him with his record so bad?
I'd say the chances were pretty slim."

So we, staunch sceptics, look at ourselves,
At our depressing history of sin,
Recognise our chronic state
And bleakly resign ourselves to fate:
"We're only being realistic," we feebly relate.

God says, "Keep your squint-eyed realism,
Your purely human calculation.
Your opinion of yourselves just doesn't interest me.
Who made the body, mind and soul, but I?
I made and can re-make, I can restore,
Make even better than before.
O ye of little faith be sure:
Your inveterate failure is not fated,
Whatever I've created
I can redeem
And have."

BOOK OF LIGHTS

Divine-illumined PRISM,
Holding and displaying
Dawn beams,
Colour-tinged dewdrops,
White radiance of noon,
Pieces of rainbow,
Shafts of sunset,
Splinters of glory,
A maze of jewels,
Glittering, pearl-strewn webs,
Love's vast, glimmering network,
Joy cubed,
Collected gleams of HEAVEN.

THE POET'S DILEMMA

Catch that fragile, fleeting intuition
And pin it down in print,
It will doubtless die
In the process
Through rough handling
With incompetent words.

Stay passive and dumb,
Let it fly away,
And you may
Never see it again.

'O FOR A MUSE ...!'
To the limited lyric poet in summer

Poems should be
Pouring out of me,
There's so much to rejoice in!

Each joy a book
Which opened
Brings page after page
Of further delights
And leads me on
To other books
With yet more pages to feed upon.

But profusion
Defeats the poet's pen,
He cannot corral
Such teeming life:
Single joys or griefs
Are what he best excels in

And to celebrate
A dazzling feast
Where many pleasures mass and merge
And yet remain distinct,
He must strike a golden vein,
Resource himself
With weighty language,
Rich and versatile and rare

And where are such veins to be found now?

Maybe he should stick to sorrow:
Squeezing, pressing,
Plain and simple sorrow
Which, he knows, can wring out words
Even from a spring
Gone dry.

PERFECT COMPOSITION

Breeze bends
And sun tints yellow
The blades of grass.
What a wonderful thing
Is this bend-tinting,
This leaning and glinting together
In an easy, natural harmony.

Almost as marvellous as a wave
Of Mozart's music:
Spontaneous and pure and fresh and free,
Yet finely made,
Deliberately composed.
Subtle,
Yet utterly simple.

LENT AND ATHLETIC CHRISTIANITY

Come on board,
Join the team!
Let's train together,
Get fit not fat.
Work hard for that cup.
The road-running
Iron-pumping
Muscle-stretching
Will work wonders.

You're doing what
The Coach, the Boss wants.
He did it first,
That's why he's the Boss
And knows what's best.
His training programme is perfect,
And, what's more, he'll train
Alongside you.
So, come on, get stuck in:
Get fit not fat,
Win that cup!

The cup of suffering
Which becomes a cup of blessing,
And a cup of triumph
'At the end of the day'!

SPRING CLEAN

There remain places in our lives
We shut God out,
Thinking he cannot see
Or has no business there.
But he can see
And has every right to be there –
He made and owns everywhere

But will not visit his domains
Until we open up to him.
Throw open the shutters,
Lift the blinds,
Clear the windows,
And let in his rays.

Like a beam of sunshine
In the cellar
All the dust will come to light,
But it will be warm in there,
And, after so much murk,
O so bright!

INDIFFERENT FRIDAY – An Answer to T.S. Eliot

Easter Bank Holiday weekend. Friday.
Many have the day off, some work as usual.
Some shops are closed, some open,
But the streets are quiet and dull.
Nothing much happening.
Says one, "Fishing for me,"
Says another, "A trip to the sea with the family
Or maybe some *beauty spot*". Says a third one,
"If it stays fine a round of golf in the morning,
Bit of shopping, maybe, or wash the car.
Saturday, a potter in the garden or, if it rains, TV,
Or go online and surf the Net. Later, drink
With in-laws, no doubt. With any luck, Sunday
Will be golf again but must wash the car
If not done before, it's got quite dirty again since last week."
A fourth one says, whilst still in bed,
"I'll be up by eleven then share a midday jar
With Pete and Jo at The Boar. A drive
In the afternoon, perhaps, or tinker with the car.
Then the telly, then The Boar again
With or without my partner. Saturday a bit different:
Odd jobs about the house, watching sport on Sky TV.
Sunday much the same as today I hope. Monday
I'll take it easy." He rolls over, dozing happily.

Four simple folk, maybe thousands like them.
Ordinary, probably suburban folk,
Yet abused and assailed by some literary men.
Talked of in terms of *death*. Is this fair?
These people know nothing of death.
They may be said to sleep a little
But are not dead. T.S. Eliot, for one,
Has got it wrong, surely. These neutral beings,
Amongst whom have we all been numbered in our way,
Are not hiding from their 'dust'.
They're merely resting satisfied with small things.
Not 'hollow men', 'stuffed men', just plain people
Who know not what they don't do.
Oh, Eliot is too hard on them; he wrongly despises
Those simple pleasures of their modest existence.
Do they mean Death? Wasn't he able to appreciate

(And he a religious man) the 'common task'
Of washing the car at weekends, the humble, homely pint,
The 'trivial round' of golf on a Saturday or Sunday,
The pleasure of the firm feel of the turf
Beneath a firm golf shoe, the invigorating breeze
Blowing across the course? Could he never enjoy
A holy day, which is, after all, a holiday?

Yet holy day, holiday, holyday?
Which is it now? Have we taken the holiday
And abandoned the holyday,
Holy day? These simple pleasures are not Death, no,
But are we capable of no more,
Is this all we were made for?
The ignoring of deeper things is not Death,
But is it Life?

Dying we cannot evade, can no one, but Death
We need not face. We are quite at liberty
To stay on the safe, familiar shore,
Appearing to move at our own pace, and look out at
Adventures on, and drownings in, the sea,
As a child watches boats on a pond.
We need not even look.
Let things go smoothly all the way:
Let the quiet ticking of a clock
Mirror the steady rhythm of our simple existence.
Let not one day seem too different from another.
Friday is always 'good' in one way because
It is the end of the working week. This Friday
Is deader than most and a sort of holiday
But apart from that what can you say about this Friday?
It comes after Thursday and before Saturday, that's all.

And someone who does know, the Unseen Enemy, who has set
This tempo and circuit of thought for many,
Although they simply do not know it, he whispers to us,
    "Let us keep to the even, known ground.
    Let us not sink low nor rise high.
    Not for us despair, great sorrow; nor for us great hope or joy,
    Not for us deep suffering; nor for us uplifting glory.
    Not for us the sense of failure; nor for us the triumph.

Not for us the excruciating conflict; nor the all-mastering harmony.
Not for us the harrowing soul-searching, the overpowering, dizzying deeps,
The breathless, staggering, ungraspable riches of *Good* Friday;
Nor the firm feel of a rediscovered land,
The re-freshening air of a new world,
The brilliant clarity, the astonishing clutchability of Easter Day.

Not for us Crucifixion, Resurrection;
Death, Life".

VOICES

Voices, always I hear voices,
Telling me what I should, shouldn't do,
Telling me I'll fail, I'll never change,
So there's no point in trying.

The sniggering, scoffing voices I hear
Whenever I pray or try to reform.
So insistent, unrelenting, so often right,
Damn them!
I can see them laughing too,
The faces behind the voices.
If only I could smash their smirking faces,
Grind them into the ground
And stomp all over them, those grinning devils!

Where are the angelic voices,
The divine promptings,
The gentle calls and whispers from above?
Fallen asleep on the job, have they, those angels,
Our appointed guardians?
Or has the cacophony of demonic voices
Drowned them out?

Speak to me, Lord, directly.
Help me to re-tune to you,
Cutting out the alien airwaves,
All that diabolical interference!

Let your signal come through
Loud and clear.

Speak, Lord,
Now, I pray,

And let your servant hear.

PUTTING ON YOUR ARMOUR

Step into God's will,
Into his beam of grace and truth,
He will clothe you
And irradiate you
With the power of his risen Son,

He will circle you round
And shield you
From the darts
Of the Evil One.

Step into God's Kingdom,
Into his marvellous light.
Spread out to left and right,
Be ready for the fight,
For delight,
Greater love, more insight.

Step into God's Light
And *stay there*.

That's prayer.

THE PROBLEM OF ANSWERED PRAYER

I knocked on the door
And to my surprise
Someone came.
I was half hoping
No one would come,
That I'd be able to go away and say,
"I tried but no one was in".

Yet Someone came.
That's awkward –
I'll have to stay
And listen now
And maybe enter in.

EXHORTATIONS
AND MAXIMS

DEPRESSION

Depression is a deadly thing,
Don't give it any scope;
Let it have an inch of gloom,
It'll take a yard of hope.

SIW (SELF-INFLICTED WORRY)

Life is like a pane of glass on which we breathe
And wonder why it clouds.

BE NOT ANXIOUS

Worries hover round us
In a gathering grey mist,
They haunt us, they hound us,
They threaten to confound us.
We try to forget them, ignore them, deny them,
We busy ourselves, we hurry on by them,
But the sidelong glance, the fleeting, furtive glimpse,
Remind us they're still there,
And when we turn our eyes away
They only weigh on us the more.
Like the child's ghosts and monsters
That hide behind the bedroom door
Or lurk beneath the bed,
Their presence is the more confirmed
Every time she will not look.

Yes, the more we evade them and avoid them,
The more we cower,
The more they grow:
Our cringing gives them space to spread
And magnifies them.

Who casts these mounting clouds on us,
What is it that we fear?
When we turn and look them in the face,
And, by God's grace,
See them clear
In the beam of his truth,
They shrink, they disappear.

HOPE AND EXPECTATION

Wait for the probable, look for the probable, expect the probable,
And only the probable will ever happen to you,
The improbable wish come true will be missed.
Like the shaft of sudden sunlight
Breaking through the grey,
Just when we've given up our half-hearted hope
And gone away.

BE POSITIVE

Yes, grey days will come
But what are grey days for
But to be made bright?
Those dark, oppressive clouds above,
So stubborn and unmoving,
Are no less transient
Than any of your short-lived joys
And will go. If not, the Sun
Will punch a hole in them
With his jubilant, thrusting fist!

GOD IS THERE

'There is no night
Only the world is turning
From the light'. (Irene Gough)

Never say that God's not there
Or that he's doing nothing.
Like his sun he pours out power perpetually,
Whilst we,
Like the globe at night,
Turn from him,
Or let clouds of cares and affairs
Blot out the *sight* of his rays.

GRACE FAVOURS THE BRAVE

Shrink not back from those shadows round the corner.
Run to meet them, shake them by the hand,
Smile into their faceless face and see
A look take shape that's not of malice.
Who knows? You'll make friends of them yet,
Find their threat's turned into a blessing
By the working of God's grace.

GRACE AND TRUTH

Fear not to tread the untrodden path ahead,
Life is not to be feared but enjoyed.
God in Christ has opened up a new perspective,
Gone on ahead, prepared the way for us,
And sent back his Sun
To lead us into all truth.

WORTH WAITING FOR

The buried seed lies underground
In total darkness
And its growth cannot be seen,
But faith knows it's begun.
One day, a plant,
It *will* break the surface,
Encounter the light,
Breathe the air
And feel the warm sun.

THE SCOPE OF HAPPINESS

Never narrow down the sphere of your happiness,
Turn everything to good account.
Squeeze some juice from the driest times,
Then watch your joys: see how they mount!

FAITH AND REASON

Reason is looking at truth from a distance,
Faith is actually going there.

EXCUSES FOR FEEBLE ENDEAVOUR

Between 'when I am older' and 'if I were younger'
Lie the wasted years. For which we can, probably,
Blame no one but ourselves.

MAKE THE MOST OF IT

When the wind is against you, keep running,
And when it's behind you, you'll fly.
If you don't run well when the wind is behind you,
When it's against you, you might not be able to walk.

SONG: Trusting God

Go forth in peace
Into life before you,
Christ's been ahead of you
Of that you can be sure.

Go forth in faith,
Trusting in God's promises,
He knows the power you need
And he will supply it.

You mustn't hurry
For it only makes you worry,
You'll get there be sure, my friend,

If you take life steady,
You will find that you are ready
To meet what comes your way,

Just do your best and leave the rest
In the capable hands of God.

DIVERTISSEMENTS

UPLIFT

A little sun came up
Above a miniature horizon –
My son's head above the top of his cot.
More heart-warming and marvellous, to me,
Than any dawn ever.

DETECTED

"Hey, look, Dad's got paint in his hair,
White paint!" I laughed, "Must be the decorating
They're doing at work," I said,
But no one was decorating there.

Mind you, I thought, I'll need to do
Some decorating now, oh yes.
For that's not paint my sharp daughter saw,
That's age!

A LA CAMPAGNE: THE FORETASTE

Just to breathe the morning air,
Its clearness and its freshness;
Just to smell the dew-soaked fields,
To feel the cool warmth all around you;
Just to hear the silence, not quite silence,
But every sound you hear belongs
And fortifies the stillness;
Just to see the red sun glimmering through the morning mist
Heralding a glorious day;
Just to know there are friends nearby
To share this peace and the feast to come
Is enough. For this life.

(Inspired by the stay at Le Clôteau, near Mansigné, Vallèe du Loir, August 1994).

French version

A LA CAMPAGNE: L'AVANT-GOUT

Rien que de respirer l'air du matin,
 toute pureté, toute fraicheur;
Rien que de sentir l'odeur des prés trempés de rosée,
 sentir cette fraiche tiédeur;
Rien que d'écouter le silence, pas tout à fait le silence:
 mais chaque bruit que l'on entend
 Appartient à cette tranquillité et la renforce;
Rien que de voir le soleil, rougissant à travers
 la brume matinale, (bien) annoncant une journée merveilleuse;
Rien que de savoir les amis tout près
 partageant ce calme et la promesse de fête:
Tout cela suffit. Pour cette vie-ci.

THINGS WHICH LAST

Endued with a massive and monumental calm,
The mountains endure.
The rocks, the hills, the crags,
Whether clouds crown them for an hour
Or mists cloak them for days,
Whether winds beat them or snows cover them,
They endure.
The trees endure:
Whether in straggling copses or full forests
Or clinging singly to mountainsides,
They endure.
The sparse green fields endure
And their sheep and grey stone walls,
They endure despite the weather.
The gullies, glens and gorges endure
And their streams; their rivers and their brooks
Which make ceaseless conversation to the indifferent sky,
They endure.
The bleak and half-hidden tarns endure,
The flat and placid lakes endure
And the mountains watching over them,
The rocks and the hills and the crags ...
All these endure,
And the RAIN.

THE BANE OF SCOTLAND

The huge bulk and massive menace of encircling mountains;
Gales, driving rain and blizzards, blanket mists
And thunder, freezing ice and falling snow,
All Nature's hardware, her heavy artillery,
Daunt not the intrepid walker,
The steely outdoorman.

But Nature's nothings,
Barely tangible,
Almost invisible,
Dithering, dancing dots in the air,
They taunt and intimidate far more.

Midges!

Miniscule, hovering phantoms,
They haunt more stubbornly
Than any avenging ghost;
Guerilla enemies,
Sly terrorists,
For a time gone to ground,
And then, when it's still,
Hounding, baiting, harassing humans
Without remorse.

Of no corporeal weight or power,
Mere pinpricks their weaponry,
Puny essences, of no might at all,
Yet they imprison people indoors
More surely than any besieging army
Or military curfew.

Frail and ephemeral
As dandelion clocks,
And yet
More feared and noticed,
These insignificant specks,
Than all the Big Bens of the Highlands!

TELL IT LIKE IT IS

So. She's passed on,
Passed away,
Fallen asleep,
Gone to meet her Maker,
Her ancestors,
Rejoin her loved ones?

No, no, no!
Don't beat about the bush,
Call a spade a spade!
She's lost her battle with old age.

SO LONG, FADE WELL

"We'll miss you, old boy,
What a hole you'll leave in all of our lives!"
"Don't know how we'll manage without you:
You're irreplaceable, quite irreplaceable!"
"Yes, things will never be the same without you, old boy,
Never!"

"Of course his contribution was always exaggerated,
He didn't do all that much, you know."
"But he played his part."
"Oh yes, a small part, while he was here."

"Do you remember old ... ?"
"Not really. What did he do?"
"Oh, this and that, I believe."

"Whatever happened to what's his name?"
"Don't know: lost touch some years ago."

"Can you remember old, you know ... ?"
"Who?"

THERE IS A TIDE

"Sail with me, come sail with me,
Sail away!"

"Yes, I would like to sail,
I really would like to sail,
Sail away ...

Some day ... some day."

BROTHER ANDREW

Awake, Brother Andrew, awake!
The risen sun your strength renews.
Awake, arise, be swift,
Action and thought now fuse!

Another chance you have now
To use your wit,
Be, live, do, before you lose it,
Brother Andrew.

Now start again and end
Your meddling with muddling philosophies
Which bemuse
You so: wipe out your hazy views.

Wipe out and start again,
For now you must act!
No longer can you excuse
Yourself with 'if there were time, perhaps, perhaps',
There is time and you cannot refuse,
Brother Andrew.

Oh yes, you've drifted your time away
When your time you could misuse,
But now it's over – the trip nowhere, the cruise –
Brother Andrew.

Those great works just haven't come, my friend,
Though you've ruminated long in numerous queues,
And many's the time you've sat pondering in pews,
Brother Andrew.

Brother Andrew, another day has gone
And you've done nothing!
If with tomorrow's sun wakes your muse,
May I be first to hear the news,
Mon frère.

IF YOU CAN'T BEAT IT ...

Time slips
Through your hands
Like running water
There's no holding it
Better plunge
Into its flow
Let it carry
You along
Enjoy
The sensation
And the changing
Scene
You will reach
Your destination
Maybe late
Or soon
Trust God
Do His will
So as you
Move
You will be
Still
Already
I am further
On
A little bit
More
Downstream
Than when
I first said
'Time slips
Through
Your hands
Like running
Water'
And I'm
Moving
Freely
With it
Now

JOURNEY BETWEEN TWO COUNTRIES
Ou t'en vas-tu, Eurostar?

Time, you do not frighten me,
Though you do alarm me somewhat,
The way you whisk me along so fast;
Nor you, Death, standing waiting
Down the line
In the ever-diminishing distance,
Your black mouth opening
Ever wider as I approach you.
You may swallow
But you cannot devour me,
For I know you are only a tunnel
To another land beyond.

FAITH'S BEGINNING (John 1, 38-46)

Does that ancient path really lead somewhere,
Is there really a land beyond the hills?

Are those promises true or just a mirage,
Is there really a place for us at the end?

Has the Lord of Life been that way before,
And can we still travel in his company?

Come and see.